Nevada
The Silver State

Marcia Amidon Lusted

PowerKiDS
press™
New York

Published in 2011 by The Rosen Publishing Group, Inc.
29 East 21st Street, New York, NY 10010

First Edition

Editor: Maggie Murphy
Book Design: Greg Tucker
Photo Researcher: Jessica Gerweck

Photo Credits: Cover, pp. 7, 9, 13, 19, 22 (flower, animal, flag, bird, reptile) Shutterstock.com; p. 5 Ron and Patty Thomas/Getty Images; p. 11 © Charles A. Blakeslee/age fotostock; p. 15 © Inga Spence/ age fotostock; p. 17 © SuperStock/age fotostock; p. 22 (Winnemucca) Wikimedia Commons; p. 22 (Reid) Nicholas Kamm/AFP/Getty Images; p. 22 (Kyle and Kurt Busch) Harry How/Getty Images.

Library of Congress Cataloging-in-Publication Data
Lusted, Marcia Amidon.
  Nevada : the Silver State / Marcia Amidon Lusted. — 1st ed.
     p. cm. — (Our amazing states)
  Includes index.
  ISBN 978-1-4488-0659-1 (library binding) — ISBN 978-1-4488-0750-5 (pbk.) —
ISBN 978-1-4488-0751-2 (6-pack)
  1. Nevada—Juvenile literature. I. Title.
  F841.3.L87 2011
  979.3—dc22
                                    2009047350

Manufactured in the United States of America

CPSIA Compliance Information: Batch #WS10PK: For Further Information contact Rosen Publishing, New York, New York at 1-800-237-9932

Contents

Welcome to Nevada!

There is a state where you can find both old mining towns and big cities. You can see ancient rock carvings, watch a camel race, and even drive on the **Extraterrestrial** Highway. Where are you? You are in Nevada!

Nevada is located in the western part of the United States. It is bordered on its western and southwestern sides by California. The Colorado River and the Hoover Dam are found in the state's southeastern corner.

The word *nevada* means "snowfall" in Spanish. The tops of Nevada's mountains are snowy from autumn through early summer. Nevada is called the Silver State because so much silver has been found there.

Here you can see snow on top of the Ruby Mountains in early spring. The Ruby Mountains are located near Elko, Nevada.

Silver Strikes and Ghost Towns

Over 12,000 years ago, the first Native Americans lived in Nevada. Some of them left behind rock carvings called petroglyphs. The first white men there were Spanish explorers and fur trappers. By the 1840s, many **pioneers** came to Nevada in covered wagons, looking for farmland and gold.

In 1859, silver and gold were found in the Comstock **Lode**, near Virginia City, Nevada. Towns where the miners could live were built quickly. However, they were deserted when miners stopped finding silver. These towns became ghost towns.

Nevada joined the United States in 1864, during the **Civil War**. This is why the words "battle born" are part of Nevada's flag. Nevada became the thirty-sixth state in the nation.

Ancient Native Americans carved these petroglyphs into rock at the Grapevine Canyon, in southern Nevada.

A Dam and a Lake

In 1931, the United States started to build a dam on the Colorado River. It would store water and make **electricity** for the dry western states. The dam, which reaches from Nevada to Arizona, is called the Hoover Dam.

The Hoover Dam took six years to build. Workers had to dig tunnels through rock cliffs and pour tons (t) of concrete to construct it. Once it was in place, the river water that slowly collected behind the dam became Lake Mead.

Today many people visit the Hoover Dam. They can go inside it or climb to the **observation deck** overlooking the dam and the lake. Lake Mead is a popular place for boating and swimming.

These are two of the Hoover Dam's four water towers. The water that enters these towers is used to turn turbines, or motors, that make electricity.

Dry Deserts and Snowy Mountains

Nevada has both dry deserts and snowy mountaintops. Most of Nevada, except for the southern part of the state, is part of the Great Basin Desert. Southern Nevada has the Mojave Desert. Very little rain falls there. As in most desert areas, Nevada can get very hot during the day and very cold at night.

The Shoshone and Ruby Mountains are in Nevada. The Sierra Nevada reach from California into the very western edge of Nevada. Rain and snow fall in the mountains.

Nevada has several big lakes, including Lake Mead, on the Colorado River, and Lake Tahoe, on the border with California. Many people visit the Lake Tahoe area for swimming, boating, and skiing.

Here you can see the sagebrush that grows in the Great Basin Desert in Nevada. The desert also covers half of Utah and parts of California, Idaho, Oregon, and Wyoming.

A Land of Sagebrush and Sheep

Plants commonly found in deserts, such as cacti, yuccas, and Joshua trees, grow in Nevada. The state flower is the blossom of the sagebrush bush, which has tiny yellow and white flowers in the spring. Piñon and bristlecone pines, junipers, and aspen trees grow on Nevada's mountain slopes.

Nevada has many different kinds of animals. Large animals include black bears, mule deer, antelope, and jackrabbits. Desert iguanas, horned lizards, geckos, and rattlesnakes are found in dry areas.

Nevada's state animal is the desert bighorn sheep. This sheep can live in the desert because it can go for long periods without water. Its hooves help it climb rocky, steep slopes.

Juniper and yucca grow in the rocky soil at the Red Rock Canyon National Conservation Area, near Las Vegas, Nevada.

13

Made in Nevada

Many different things are made and grown in Nevada. Farmers grow grains, alfalfa, melons, and vegetables. Ranchers raise cattle and sheep. Many people in Nevada work mining **minerals** like gold, silver, and copper.

Companies in Nevada make parts for aircraft engines and computers, plastics, concrete, and cement. There are even companies that make saddles and other tools for working cowboys. Companies like Amazon.com and Porsche have huge **warehouses** in Nevada.

Many people in Nevada are part of the service **industry**. This means that they work in hotels, restaurants, and other places that provide food, places to stay, and things to do for visitors.

These sheep are grazing in the snow in northern Nevada. Sheep ranchers in Nevada raise the animals for meat, milk, and wool.

Come to Carson City

Nevada's capital is Carson City. It was named after Kit Carson, a famous scout who once explored the area. Because it was built near some of Nevada's silver mines, it was a trading post and **frontier** town for many early pioneers and miners. Carson City became the state capital in 1864.

There are many things to do in Carson City. It has several museums, including the Nevada State Museum. This museum is located in the old Carson City Mint building. You can see coins that were made there and walk through a life-size model of a nineteenth-century mine. At the Nevada State Railroad Museum, visitors can see **restored** steam engines and rail road cars. On certain weekends, they can even take a train ride around the museum.

This locomotive, or first train car, which pulls the cars, was built in 1878. It is part of the railroad museum's collection of steam engines.

The City of Neon Lights

Nevada's biggest and most famous city is Las Vegas. It is known for its 3-mile- (5 km) long main street, called the Las Vegas Strip. At night, the strip is brightly lit by **neon** signs of all sizes and shapes. There was a famous sign built in 1959 that says Welcome to Fabulous Las Vegas, Nevada. You can still see it today!

There are many fun things for families to do in Las Vegas. There are roller coasters, singing cowgirls, and circuses. At the Stratosphere Tower, the X-Scream ride tips visitors over the edge of the tower, 1,000 feet (305 m) above the street. There is also the Shark Reef at Mandalay Bay, an **aquarium** with more than 2,000 animals.

There is a replica, or copy, of the Eiffel Tower, a famous tower in Paris, France, at the Paris Las Vegas hotel. This replica is about half the size of the original.

Something for Everyone

Whether you like the bright lights of Las Vegas or the quiet ghost towns from the old mining days, Nevada has something for you. Maybe you would like to drive along the Extraterrestrial Highway, which many people claim is visited by UFOs. You could also visit Lehman Caves and see amazing limestone caverns.

In Virginia City, you can watch the International Camel Races. Camels were once used to carry salt and mail across Nevada, but today you can see them racing around a dirt track. In Reno, watch hundreds of hot-air balloons take off during the Great Reno Balloon Race. From hot, dry deserts to snowy mountaintops and busy cities to peaceful state parks, Nevada has something for everyone!

Glossary

aquarium (uh-KWAYR-ee-um) A place where animals that live in water are kept for study and show.

Civil War (SIH-vul WOR) The war fought between the Northern and the Southern states of America from 1861 to 1865.

electricity (ih-lek-TRIH-suh-tee) Power that produces light, heat, or motion.

extraterrestrial (ek-struh-teh-RES-tree-ul) From another planet.

frontier (frun-TEER) The edge of a settled country, where the wilderness begins.

industry (IN-dus-tree) A business in which many people work and make money.

lode (LOHD) A place with metal in the ground.

minerals (MIN-rulz) Natural elements that are not animals, plants, or other living things.

neon (NEE-on) A gas that has no color or odor. Tubes filled with neon are used in electric signs.

observation deck (ab-sur-VAY-shun DEK) A place where one can look out at a view.

pioneers (py-uh-NEERZ) Some of the first people to settle in a new area.

restored (rih-STORD) Put back, returned to an earlier state.

warehouses (WER-hows-ez) Buildings in which goods are stored until they are needed.

Nevada State Symbols

**State Flower
Sagebrush
Blossom**

**State Animal
Desert Bighorn
Sheep**

State Flag

**State Bird
Mountain
Bluebird**

**State Reptile
Desert Tortoise**

State Seal

Famous People from Nevada

Sarah Winnemucca
(c. 1844–1891)
Born near Humboldt
Lake, NV
Native American
Interpreter

Harry Reid
(1939–)
Born in Searchlight, NV
U.S. Senator

Kyle and Kurt Busch
(1985– and 1978–)
Born in Las Vegas, NV
NASCAR Drivers

Nevada State Map

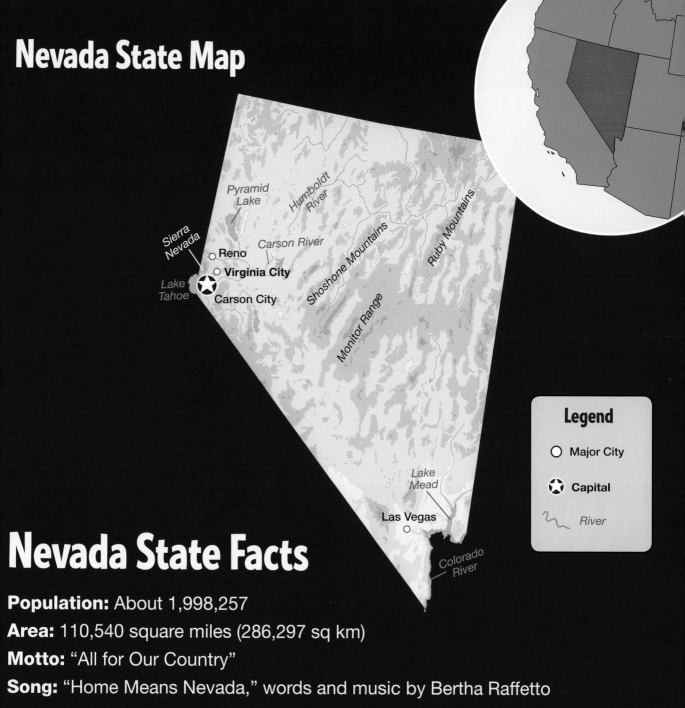

Legend

○ Major City

⍟ Capital

〜 River

Pyramid Lake

Humboldt River

Sierra Nevada

○ Reno

○ **Virginia City**

Carson River

Shoshone Mountains

Ruby Mountains

Lake Tahoe

⍟ Carson City

Monitor Range

Lake Mead

Las Vegas
○

Colorado River

Nevada State Facts

Population: About 1,998,257

Area: 110,540 square miles (286,297 sq km)

Motto: "All for Our Country"

Song: "Home Means Nevada," words and music by Bertha Raffetto

Index

Web Sites

Due to the changing nature of Internet links, PowerKids Press has developed an online list of Web sites related to the subject of this book. This site is updated regularly. Please use this link to access the list:
www.powerkidslinks.com/amst/nv/